THE TENNYSON FAMILY

AND THEIR VILLAGES

JOHN LARGE

The author acknowledges as a source "The Tennyson Album" by Andrew Wheatcroft, from which some of the Tennyson information is derived.

THE TENNYSONS

ALFRED LORD TENNYSON (1809 – 1892)

GRANDFATHER GEORGE

The Tennyson family came originally from The Tennyson family came originally from Yorkshire, but they started moving south by short steps from about 1700. Alfred's grandfather, George Tennyson, bought a small 17th century manor house called The Beacons at Tealby, near Market Rasen, in 1783. He was an attorney at Market Rasen who was respected and even feared by his clients. His clerks were terrified of him, for he had a violent temper and a reputation for being difficult.

George Tennyson's obsessions in life were money, his own health and the ingratitude and disobedience of his family. It was his ambition to be accepted in the top social circles, but he never was. He was also proud, unbending and ruthless, and the way he treated two of his children was unpardonable. Apart from Tealby he owned land at Grimsby through his uncle and his wife Elizabeth, daughter of a Grimsby merchant.

Their first son was George Clayton, Alfred's father, and both he and their second daughter Mary were sent off to be brought up by separate grandparents when little more than infants. Meanwhile, his second son Charles and first daughter Elizabeth remained at home. All plans for the future of the estate were fixed on Charles, while George's mother made no secret of her preference, either. "I think I never saw a child so rude and ungovernable," she remarked about her elder son.

Poor Mary never recovered from this banishment. She grew up to be bitter and acerbic, and although she married John Bourne and lived at Dalby, only a short drive from her brother's rectory at Somersby, the family seldom visited her. She once remarked to her nephew Alfred, "Alfred, when I look at you I think of the words of Holy Scripture: 'Depart from me, ye cursed, into everlasting fire!'" Not surprisingly, she became a rigid Calvinist.
Elizabeth, on the other hand, was a very popular aunt, whom the Somersby children referred to as Aunt Russell. She married Matthew Russell, son of a wealthy colliery owner, and lived at Brancepeth Castle, near Durham. Her husband enlarged the castle in the Gothic style with help from his brother-in-law Charles, and Charles used the experience when he came to rebuild his own estate later.

Years afterwards, Alfred used to write her heart-felt letters from Cambridge, clearly feeling that in her he had an understanding friend as well as an aunt. She sounds quite a character. She once caught her head-dress alight when lighting a candle, and promptly rang for the footman.

"William, I am on fire," she announced.

The footman earned full marks for unperturbability but none for initiative when he replied, "Very good, madam. I will go and tell Amy."

FATHER GEORGE CLAYTON

George Clayton also showed signs of his early abandonment. He grew up to be a rebel, and as he was 6 feet 2 inches in height there were not many who cared to remonstrate against him. At Cambridge he once fired a pistol shot through the window of Trinity College Chapel, which must be a unique cause for celebrity for a future clergyman of the Church of England.

After he transferred to St. John's College he was informed by his father that he should prepare for a career in holy orders, despite having neither the vocation nor aptitude for the priesthood.

George Clayton decided upon one last fling after Cambridge so took himself off to Russia. There he dined at St. Petersburg with the British Consul, Lord St. Helens, and a collection of aristocratic Russians. The conversation turned to the fate of various Russian emperors, and at one point Tennyson interposed with: "It is perfectly well known in England who murdered the Emperor Paul. It was Count X."

The table froze in horrified silence and the meal came to a hasty conclusion. Tennyson was then ushered aside by his host and informed that the very same Count X had been sitting next to him. His only chance was to leave right away and ride for his life. So George Clayton packed his scanty belongings and headed his horse out of town at a gallop under the frosty sky.

He rode for weeks, sleeping in woodmen's huts and eating whatever he could beg or purchase at the crude market stalls along the way. Eventually he arrived in the Crimea, where he literally fell from his horse, suffering badly from fever. A primitive group of villagers took pity on him, gave him floor space in a hut and nursed him through the weeks of his illness. In his delirium he was vaguely conscious of wild dancing round his bed and of magical spells being incanted above his head.

The youthful will to live was so acute that even in his semi-conscious state he was obsessed by a rumour he had heard, concerning an English courier who passed that way every three months and blew a horn as he entered the village. After many days of tossing and turning he heard the horn through his delirium, staggered out of the hut and persuaded the courier to take him with him on his journey back to England. It is a remarkable story, and not one he is likely to have related in later years to the diocesan synod!

George Clayton was ordained deacon in 1801 and priest eighteen months later. He married Elizabeth Fytche, daughter of the Vicar of Louth, a noted beauty who had already turned down 25 proposals of marriage. She was to produce a child every year from 1806 till 1819, save on three occasions. All the children survived except the first, George, who died in infancy.

This was the age when pluralities were rife in the Church of England so it was possible to hold several incumbencies at once, and thus enjoy several stipends, a curate being employed to undertake the parochial work. Father George had already procured for George Clayton the livings of Benniworth and Great Grimsby, and in 1808 the joint benefice of Somersby and Bag Enderby was added. He threw in an allowance of £140 per annum, so the new incumbent at Somersby Rectory was able to start out on his ecclesiastical career without financial hardship.

Even so, there were bitter arguments over repairs and extensions to the house. As the family and household grew at an alarming rate, the rectory soon became hopelessly inadequate. The second child, Frederick, was born at Louth in 1807 and lived to be 91. He obtained a gold medal for a Greek ode at Cambridge and was still writing poetry 70 years later, publishing a book of verse the year before he died.

The other children were all born at Somersby. Charles, the third child, won the Bell Scholarship at Cambridge, and lived to be 71. Alfred was the fourth child, lived to be 83, and not to be outdone by his elder brothers, won the English Verse prize at Cambridge. Then followed Mary, who lived to be 74, Emilia (78), Edward (77), Arthur (85), Septimus (51), Matilda (who was still alive in 1913, aged 98), Cecilia (92) and Horatio (80).

He children inherited their literary abilities from their father, who wrote good verse himself. Their grandmother Mary, who originated from the Turner family at Caistor, claimed that Alfred achieved all his poetical fame through her. But the father, George Clayton, was a considerable scholar of the Classics at Cambridge, despite his antics with gunshots through chapel windows, and he acquired a good library at Somersby, which was much used by the children.

Alfred would often take out a book and tramp through the lanes with it, lost in a world of his own, for he was an avid reader. The winter snows would be no deterrent. On one occasion he was so immersed in what he was reading that he failed to hear the Louth mail coach approaching, the hooves of the horses muffled by the snow. He was eventually roused from his reverie by a shout from the coachman, and looking up he saw a horse`s muzzle protruding over his shoulder as if it, too, was immersed in his book!

The boys were tall and striking like their father, and the girls were renowned for their good looks, particularly Mary, who was a very beautiful girl. But the parish thought them a mad household, and the cook once remarked in Alfred`s hearing, "If you raked out hell with a small tooth comb, you wouldn`t find their likes!"

EARLY YEARS AT SOMERSBY

Alfred was born in 1809, and even as a young boy he was extremely impressionable. Before he could read he would go into the rectory garden during a storm, spread his arms and declare, "I hear a voice that`s speaking in the wind!"

When he was seven he was sent to join his elder brothers Frederick and Charles at Louth Grammar School, where he remained for four years. He stayed with a relative at Harvey`s Court, a narrow alleyway in the town, before becoming a boarder at The Lodge, a large house at the bottom of Edward Street. George Clayton missed his boys so much that for a while he took rooms in Louth in order to see something of them during term-time. The boys hated the school for the headmaster was notorious for his use of the birch, and years later Alfred would never walk down Schoolhouse Lane when visiting the town.

But the boys did acquire a sound classical education. At the age of ten Alfred mastered Pope`s "Homer" and wrote hundreds of lines in imitation. This was followed by 6,000 lines based on Walter Scott. By the time he was 14 he had completed a play in blank verse.

The children used to play complex games of invasion in the rectory garden and surrounding fields, involving stone-throwing attackers and equally ruthless defenders. They always looked scruffy, and Alfred in particular was renowned for his down-at-heel appearance, with a mop of unruly dark hair which was seldom washed or brushed. None of them had any real regard for fashion, although they did mix socially to some extent for they attended dances at Spilsby and Horncastle.

The daughter of a neighbouring landowner was probably being rather generous when she wrote of the family: "The Tennysons are not easy to describe. There was both a natural grandeur and simplicity about them; a streak of impish mischief and a love of the gruesome. Delightfully unconventional, they were never like ordinary people; even their dress and walk seemed different."

For a while the three older boys attended the village school, a rough old building which had once been the village bath-house. It was closed by the farmer who owned the land, as he claimed the boys were disturbing his pheasants!

Alfred had a reputation as the strongest boy in the two villages. One of the local sports was to throw the crowbar, and at this he could beat all-comers. Later on, he once amused the household and guests by carrying a Shetland pony around the rectory lawn. He also kept a pet snake in his ever-changing menagerie.

Alfred and Charles were constant companions and used to delight in holding the bridge over Somersby brook against the village boys, a kind of Horatius exploit. They reckoned on being able to defend it against an invading force of up to five, but if the enemy numbers swelled beyond this figure, it usually ended in a ducking.

The family often took their holidays at Mablethorpe, in the same whitewashed cottage on the beach, which is now the oldest house in the town. Alfred loved the changing moods of the sea, and the wide expanses of sea, sky and sand here were frequently referred to in his early poetry. Years later, when he could afford a house of his own, he bought one with a sea view in the Isle of Wight, but he always maintained that the southern seas were a pale shadow of those that washed the Lincolnshire coast.

J. Cumin Walters refers to the Mablethorpe cottage in his book "In Tennyson Land", published in 1889. He wrote: "It is a curious home, reached by a little bridge across the stream, long and low-roofed, with four rooms leading into eachother and below. It is a peaceful spot too; nothing could be heard but the roll of the incoming tide and the swish of scythes."

Alfred himself referred to it in his "Ode to Memory":
> "Or even a lowly cottage whence we see
> Strech'd wide and wild the waste enormous marsh,
> Where from the frequent bridge,
> Like emblems of infinity,
> The trenched waters run from sky to sky."

The Tennyson family also used to holiday at Skegness, then a small fishing village, along with the Rawnsley family from Halton Holegate, for the two rectors were close friends. Skegness was then popular with the wealthier Lincolnshire families who would descend on the village in their buggies with their servants.

The children would run wild on the beach in their bare feet from dawn till dusk, and were well known to the fishermen and coastguards, some of whom had fought with Nelson. Years later, Canon H.D. Rawnsley, the son of Alfred's great friend whose father was rector of Halton Holegate, happened to call at a particularly isolated farmhouse near Gibraltar Point. The conversation turned to how the earwigs were destroying the pear crop, and how nobody liked pears more than Mr. Alfred when he used to call as a boy.

Canon Rawnsley relates in his biography "Memories of the Tennysons" how the conversation continued:

"Ivvery one, in them daays, knew Mr. Alfred hereabout howivver. You've heard tell of Mr. Alfred Tennyson, the owd Doctor's son, straange friend of owd Mr. Rownsley? He was straangen fond o' the jam as well as the pears, was Mr. Alfred. My missus ud say, 'Now here's Mr. Alfred a-cooming; we must git the jam ready'; and she would open the door and let the cat out, for he was a regular boy for the cats was Mr. Alfred. I remember our cat, poor thing, went up smoke-hole one time when he coomed in at the door, and Mr. Alfred said, 'Your cats is so shan, Mrs. G.' and like enough, poor things. Not that he meant owt, but cats is sensible things and they know who' who mind ye. We haven't heard tell of him for years, but he grew up a straangen great man, I suppoase, and addles his bread by his writings; is worth some hundreds, they do saay."

Rawnsley replied that Mr. Alfred was now worth thousands, not hundreds, and that the Queen wished to make him a Lord for his work as a poet. This started the old man off again.

"Missus, do you hear what this young gentleman is saying about Mr. Alfred?" he shouted through the kitchen door. "He saays he's wurth thousands by his potry! Naay, naay, sir, you mun be mistaen; sewerly it's hundreds, not thousands. Well I nivver! He was allus ramblin' off –

-11-

quite by hissen, wi'out a coat on his back and wi'out a hat on his head, nor owt.

"I remember as it wur nobbut yisterdaay, my man, as was a fiddler bit of a

fellow, was off to Hildred's theer at Skegnest, to play for quality at a dance; and he was cooming hoam in the morning early, and, be-dashed, who should he light on but Mr. Alfred, a ravin' and taavin' upon the sandhills in his shirt-sleeves an' all; and Mr. Alfred said, saays he, 'Good morning,' and my man says, 'Thou poor fool, thou doesn't knaw morning from night,' for you know, sir, I' them days we all thought he was crazed. Well, well! And the Queen wants to make him a Lord, poor thing! Well, I nivver did hear the likes o' that for sarten sewerness."

At home in Somersby, Alfred shared a room with a window in the gable, at the top of the rectory. Here he used to sit and write, listening to the sounds of the night outside. He once answered the hoot of an owl with such authenticity that the bird flew into the room. It became so tame that it would sit by him while he wrote, rubbing its beak against his face.

Alfred shared with his mother Elizabeth a love of all wild animals. He had an aversion to the traps which the gamekeepers used to set for foxes and other vermin, and made a habit of springing them, much to the annoyance of the gamekeepers. They told him that if they ever caught him in the act, they would duck him in the village pond, but such threats would have carried little menace for the young naturalist.

Presiding over the domestic side of this wild household was their mother Elizabeth, a small, gentle, very beautiful woman who was idolised by her children. She put up with the noise, the continual pregnancies, the eventual family of fourteen in a draughty rectory that was bulging at the seams, the house guests and the moods of depression and sometimes outright hostility from her husband with scarcely a murmur, giving the family a free rein to express themselves as they would.

She kept a monkey and various other pets, which had the run of the rectory and its garden. The more spirited lads of the two villages soon found out that the quickest way to earn a penny was to beat a dog underneath her window, whereupon she would immediately rush out and hand over the coin on condition that they stopped.

As for George Clayton, whom the surrounding area referred to as the Doctor, he soon discerned that his studious and erudite sermons were wasted on his Sunday flock of agricultural labourers, gamekeepers and their wives. He felt his talents frustrated by the intellectual poverty of the area, and he was depressed that preferment in the church did not come his way.

He was by no means the first earnest and intellectual Lincolnshire clergyman to suffer in this way. In 1711 The Rev'd. Solomon Ashbourne, vicar of Crowle, had the following message to his parishoners inscribed on his tombstone:

"Ye stiffnecked and uncircumcised in hearts and ears; ye do always resist the Holy Ghost; as your fathers did, so do ye. I have laboured in vain, I have spent my strength for naught."

At about the same time The Rev'd. Samuel Wesley, father of John and Charles, was trying his best to win over the souls of the people of Epworth. He started his ministry at South Ormsby, very close to Somersby. Sadly this good man was far too intellectual to have much effect on his congregation, huddled in their draughty pews. He too was depressed by lack of preferment within the hierarchy of the church, and his wife Susanna was moved to write:

"Did I not know that Almighty wisdom hath views and ends in fixing the bounds of our habitation which are out of our ken, I should think it a thousand pities that a man of his brightness and rare endowments of learning and of useful knowledge in relation to the church of God should be confined to a small corner of the country, where his talents are buried, and he determined to a way of life for which he is not as well qualified as I could wish."

Somersby was even more remote than Epworth, and although George Clayton was administering to his Lincolnshire flock the best part of a century later, one can sympathise with his problems. At least he found exhilaration from his family, just as Samuel Wesley had done. He also had plenty of friends.

These included The Rev'd. Drummond Rawnsley, rector of Halton Holegate, who was later a guardian of the Tennyson children. His son remained a friend of Alfred's all his life, visiting the poet years later at his home on the Isle of Wight. George Clayton was also always welcome at Harrington Hall, then still owned by the Amcott family, and the children treated its grounds as an extension of the rectory garden.

A particular friend was George Clayton's next-door neighbour, John Empringham Baumber, who lived at The Grange. Baumber was an eccentric and wealthy farmer and is reputed to be the original 'Northern Farmer' in Alfred's poem of that name, written in the Lincolnshire dialect. The two men had little in common intellectually, but found in each other's company a bond of contented companionship, and many was the pint of ale that they drank together as the shadows lengthened and the day's work was done.

By now, Alfred was being educated at home by his father, along with most of the rest of the family. Life was comfortable enough for them, and although Alfred would have been aware of the social revolution going on around him caused by the Enclosure Acts, he was well sheltered from it.

THE AGRICULTURAL REVOLUTION

In 1815 the price of wheaten flour rose to six shillings a stone. Country people made do with barley cakes, and mothers made cardboard boxes on the kitchen floor to supplement the family income. These boxes they hawked around the country markets, or offered for sale at the back doors of the bigger farmhouses.

There was a huge gap between the rich and the poor, and the Enclosure Acts increased it still further. The larger landowners set about canvassing support for the enclosure of the ancient "open fields, common and other waste ground." This was the land that the smaller freeholders and cottagers depended upon for their very existence. They were unable through lack of education and financial inability to employ lawyers to put their case to a parliamentary committee, so were literally pushed aside and deprived of their livelihoods.

The only concession made to the cottagers was the use of the verges along the roads in the Wolds, which to this day tend to be very wide. These were let out for grazing. But the days of the small independent farmer were almost over in most areas. The villages now consisted of the landowner in the big house and the farm labourers who worked for him.

Hedges were planted, drains were dug, the surveyors departed and the deed was done. The Lincolnshire Wolds, which had been used for little else apart from hunting the fox and coursing the hare, became a vast area of corn growing and sheep rearing. No new houses were built in the villages as the landowners were apprehensive about times of unemployment, when their occupants would be a financial drain. In those days before social welfare, the big landowners did consider their labourers to be part of their responsibilities.

Here were a few open villages where there was no big landowner and so houses could be built. Winterton, near Scunthorpe, was one, and this became over-crowded with farm workers who set off before dawn every morning on their donkeys to whichever farm they had current employment. Sometimes they had to ride for 15 or 20 miles before starting work.

Worse still was the lot of the women and girls, used at peak times by the large farms on the fens. Mrs. Burroughs describes in her book 'Life as We Have Known It' how she was recruited by one such gang operating near Crowland, in the south of the county, at the age of eight – and she was the oldest in the gang! They walked for miles each day to the contracted farm, worked a 14 hour shift, and then had to walk home again. Those who showed signs of fatigue felt the lash of the overseer's whip.

This horrific state of affairs was going on after the various Factory Acts had put a stop to the exploitation of child labour in the textile mills of Derbyshire, Yorkshire and Lancashire. It was really only the Forster Education Act of 1870, whereby primary school education to the age of eleven was made compulsory, which put a stop to it.

FAMILY PROBLEMS

Although the Tennyson family at Somersby was well sheltered from these goings on, their lives were by now overshadowed by the depression and violent behaviour of their father, George Clayton. His failure to obtain preferment in the church was a subsidiary cause, but the main reason for the rector's disintegration as a husband, father and priest was the treatment that was meted out to him by his father, George.

His mother appeared to have no affection for him and his father blatantly passed him over as the elder son in favour of his younger brother Charles. This abusive treatment from his parents scarred him for life, eventually breaking out into a festering sore in early middle age. Even then his father, the old lawyer from Tealby, used to taunt and ridicule him in front of his young family.

A letter he wrote to his father in 1820, when he was 43, shows only too clearly how such treatment rankled with George Clayton, right down to the deepest recesses of his soul:

"With the sentiments you yet entertain and have entertained for more than 20 years, I cannot wonder you told Mr. Bourne you had not a spark of affection for me. The rude and unprecedented manner in which you first addressed me, after a long absence, upon your return from York (I quote your own words: 'Now, you great awkward booby, are you here')... and your language and conduct in innumerable other instances, many of which have made a deep impression upon my mind, sufficiently prove the truth of your assertion."

Grandfather George from Bayons Manor did provide the family with a basic annuity which made their early years at Somersby comfortable enough. But as the family grew, their financial affairs became increasingly strained.

Partly to increase their accommodation and partly to satisfy a whim, George Clayton designed an extension to the rectory in the Gothic style. This was built by his general factotum, Mr. Horlins. Years later, one of the villagers described George Clayton as "a reet clever old chap as a harchitect," but whether his design was faulty or Mr. Horlins was not the master bricklayer he attained to be, a builder had to be brought in to solidify the building.

Horlins was one of the few people who could handle George Clayton's moods. Once, when he was reprimanded for not having cleaned the carriage harness properly, he flung it on the ground at the rector's feet and told him to do it himself.

George Clayton adorned his new hall with some very good wood carvings, and he certainly educated his sons very well. He would stand no nonsense in the schoolroom and inspired both creativity and an enthusiasm for learning. He was determined that his oldest son Frederick should suffer none of the deprivations that he had suffered as the firstborn son, so with help from his grandfather, the boy was packed off to Eton.

There he proved intelligent and quick to learn, and excelled at both cricket and football. But he had inherited some of his father's rebellious spirit, and after progressing to Cambridge he was rusticated for three terms. This not surprisingly upset his father, and bitter wrangles ensued at the rectory.

On one occasion the constable was summoned to remove Frederick from the house. His father now kept a knife and a loaded gun in the rectory, openly threatening to use them on Frederick. He was drinking heavily and started to suffer from epileptic fits. The family went through a miserable time, and Alfred would have suffered as acutely as his mother, brothers and sisters from the time he was about ten till he was 22, when his father died.

George Clayton, who had the most supportive of wives in Elizabeth, tried to arrest his own disintegration. He visited an establishment in Cheltenham which specialised in cold water treatment on several occasions and sensibly went on a prolonged tour of the Continent in 1829, which resurrected his classical learning and did him good. But poor Elizabeth his wife, who many times must have wished that she had accepted one of her other 25 proposals of marriage, wrote to a friend on his return:

"It appears to me there is but little hope of any permanent tranquility. I cannot but confess I have the greatest dread of what may happen. May God (as he has mercifully done hitherto) protect my family. You know as well as myself that when under the influence of liquor George is dreadfully violent."

So it was a relief to all when George Clayton became ill in 1831 with a strain of typhus, and died in March. One feels dreadfully sorry for the man who had so much scholarship and inclination towards good within him. Had he not been cast adrift from his parents at such a young age, so much suffering could have been avoided. He lies buried in a plain tomb in Somersby churchyard, where violets blossom on the bank every year. Neither his father George nor his brother Charles attended the funeral.

YEARS OF STRUGGLE

George Clayton had amply prepared his three elder sons for Cambridge, and both Charles and Alfred joined their eldest brother Frederick there in 1828, relieved to escape from the atmosphere at the rectory. All three were at Trinity College.

Already they were there as published poets, for two years previously Jacksons of Louth had published 'Poems by Two Brothers', although there were contributions from all three in the volume. They had received £20 from the publisher, a condition being that more than half of it was to be spent on books. Charles and Alfred went off to Mablethorpe for the day to celebrate, running and shouting their delight to the sea and the gulls.

At first, Alfred was slow to settle at Cambridge. It must be remembered that most of his fellow students had come up together from some public school or other, whereas he had rarely been further than Louth in his life. Consequently he appeared shy and reserved, disliking the flat drabness of the countryside and the sounds of drunken revelry which every night floated into his college window. He also found his studies dull after the imaginative teaching of his father, referring to the dons as "dry-headed, calculating, angular little gentlemen."

Alfred had always been a keen observer of nature, which abounded literally on his doorstep at Somersby. He had become a naturalist when still a boy, and by this stage of his life he was also a botanist of some exactitude. So one can imagine that his first taste of town life left him with a feeling of some deprivation.

Things looked up when he won the Chancellor's Medal for English Poetry with his poem 'Timbuctoo', written to a set subject. Later he scorned this work, but it caused him to be noticed within the University. Gradually he had become a member of a small group of highly intelligent students with similar interests. The group included Arthur Hallam, also a somewhat lonely figure as his Etonian friends had all gone up to Oxford. One of his contemporaries from Eton was William Gladstone, who cherished Hallam's memory all his life.

Alfred and Arthur Hallam became inseparable friends. Hallam was an idealist, a young man with great charisma. When they were together life was exciting, the future infinite, conversation flowing in a great swell of joie de vivre. Together they visited Spain and Germany in the vacations, and when Hallam came up to Somersby and fell in love with Alfred's younger sister Emily, life was just perfect. Despite opposition from Hallam's father, the two were engaged.

When George Clayton died in 1831, aged only 52, Alfred had to leave Cambridge to manage the family affairs. Then in 1833 came the shattering news that Hallam had died in Vienna. Emily and Alfred were distraught. He wrote of his whole life being shattered, and how he would prefer to die rather than to go on living. Not until his great work 'In Memoriam' was published in 1850 was his grief finally assuaged, and poor Emily never really recovered from losing her young lover.

Meanwhile, Alfred was becoming increasingly infatuated by a beautiful young lady living only two miles up the road at Harrington Hall. She was Rosa Baring, whose father had been a rich banker who had made his fortune in India. But he had drowned when she was only seven. Harrington Hall was then owned by Robert Cracroft who had let it to Arthur Eden, Rosa's guardian. She and Alfred had known eachother for some while, but Rosa was moving in a higher and much wealthier strata of society, and their earlier relationship had been no more than a flirtation.

Alfred now developed an intense passion for her which found material form in his poem 'Maud', published some 20 years later. This was savaged by the critics, one of whom saw lurking in its lines adultery, fornication, murder and suicide, no less.

Alfred realised only too well that the small sum left to him by his grandfather in 1835 would not support a wife and family, and he was conscious of his responsibilities in caring for his mother and the younger children. He showed some of George Clayton's bitterness that the family fortune had passed over his own father in favour of his Uncle Charles, who was spending it on the rebuilding of Bayons Manor. In 1838 Rosa married a rich landowner from County Durham, and so their paths separated.

UNCLE CHARLES

The family fortune did not ultimately bring peace of mind and prosperity to Uncle Charles, although life had started off so well for him. After attending schools in York, Lincoln and Louth he graduated from St. John's College, Cambridge and went off to London to work in chambers. He married Fanny Hutton, who inherited from her mother property in Yorkshire and Lincolnshire. However, Fanny was one of the many who could not get on with father-in-law George, so they moved back to London.

For a while it looked as if Charles would enjoy a glittering political career, for he became M.P. for Grimsby in 1818 and then for Stamford in a famous contest. He was made a Privy Councillor, but he never achieved the political success that was his ambition. This may partly have been because his father wanted him to give up parliament and settle down to the life of a Lincolnshire country gentleman.

Charles by now had discovered in old title deeds that his father's property Tealby Lodge had once been known as Bayons Manor, a name then adopted by the family. In 1833 old George, his father, moved the short distance to Usselby, so that Charles could move into Bayons Manor and rebuild it in a most ostentatious manner, along Gothic lines. George never lived to see the rebuilding completed, for he died in 1835.

His body was taken to Tealby for burial, accompanied by 60 men on horseback and 2,000 on foot. The bell tolled every 30 seconds for 14 hours, which cannot have endeared to the villagers their memories of the old fellow as they tried in vain to get some sleep. Few of the nobility attended the funeral, and neither did his nephews and nieces from Somersby.

The lavish amount of money which Charles spent on what was generally regarded as his Gothic folly caused it to be the subject of ridicule among the gentry, as was his claim to the d'Eyncourt title which was flawed. He claimed a connection to the great Norman barons of that name, on whom William the Conqueror lavished many Lincolnshire estates. This antagonism from the very strata of society he was attempting to emulate caused Charles considerable distress. He developed a persecution complex, and became as difficult and acerbic as his father had been. He was convinced that he was being cheated by his builders and employees.

Meanwhile, his marriage was in difficulties, and he conducted a long-standing affair with Miss Thornhill, a friend of his sister Elizabeth. Miss Thornhill came from near Bakewell in Derbyshire, and for 22 years wrote him letters addressing him as her "dearest beauty". More distress was caused to him by his oldest son George, who never recovered from the death of the girl he was in love with, Emily Lytton, and he took to drink.

Charles's second son Edwin joined the navy and did so well that he eventually became an admiral. But in his younger years he hated Bayons Manor and became abusive to his father, which resulted in their separation and his life afloat. His youthful ambition was to marry a wealthy wife and to leave what he called "a most beastly county."

The third son Eustace was his father's favourite. He entered the army, became a captain and died of fever in Barbados when only 26. His death caused his father to become increasingly disenchanted with life. He degenerated into a solitary figure, riding round his estate muttering about the futility of it all.

There were also two daughters. Julia distressed her father by becoming a Roman Catholic and eventually entering a convent. Clara was a thoroughly good-natured soul who married the local M.P. and succeeded in reuniting the Tealby and Somersby Tennysons after the death of Charles.

Meanwhile, the grandiose Bayons Manner was the talking-point of the Lincolnshire gentry. One of the Cracrofts called there in 1849 and afterwards wrote in his diary: "But that old baronial hall! And the owner the second son of a Market Rasen attorney! It is too absurd!" On a later visit he described the house as being the ridicule of the county, and wrote that its owner "has some good talk, tho' a bit of a quack, even if trying to make himself out to be a great man."

But the curate at Tealby had to be rather more circumspect regarding his chief parishioner. The Rev'd. Henry Sutton described it with a measure of Christian goodwill:

"People used to laugh at it, as an attempt to reproduce in modern times a baronial castle. I am no judge of architecture; but many and many a time, as I walked in the park, I used to look at the exquisite lines of that house, which seemed exactly to harmonise with the steep hillside on which it was built, and say to myself, 'A thing of beauty is a joy for ever.'"

Henry Sutton was often invited to dine at Bayons Manor, and enjoyed the company of such men as Lord Lytton and Sir Thomas Wise at the dinner table. He also relished the occasions when he dined alone with Charles, who would talk about his early parliamentary experiences. He described his host as a thorough man of the world – ambitious, laborious and a finished courtier. If he had an object to gain, wrote Sutton, he would never let temper, toil, trouble or want of tact interfere with its attainment.

The Tennyson d'Eyncourt family remained in residence until the last war, when Bayons Manor was occupied by the army. By 1949 it was in a sad state of decay, and passed into the hands of various farming companies. It was finally blown up in 1964, and hardly any sign of it remains today, a forlorn reminder of one man's dynasty which cost him a fortune but bought him little in the way of joy.

LIFE AFTER SOMERSBY

In 1832 a new volume of Alfred`s poetry had been published. It included such well-known poems as 'The Lady of Shalott', 'The Dream of Fair Women', 'Morte d`Arthur', 'Locksley Hall', 'The Miller`s Daughter' and 'The Lotus Eaters', all written before Alfred was 23. It was popular with the public but was ferociously reviewed by the critics.

As the years wore on after George Clayton`s death it was inevitable that the family would have to vacate the rectory at Somersby, and sure enough in 1837 the new rector required his official residence. Fortunately, a friend of Elizabeth`s lent them High Beech, a small estate overlooking Waltham Abbey in Epping Forest. Alfred, who for some time had assumed the role of head of the family, organised the move.

The family was now reduced in number, for Frederick, the oldest son, had moved to his beloved Italy. Charles, the second son, had also moved away, to become vicar and patron of Grasby, near Caistor. In the same year as the family move Charles married Louisa Sellwood, whose father was a respected Horncastle solicitor. Her mother was a sister of John Franklin, the intrepid explorer from Spilsby who discovered the North West Passage, linking the Atlantic with the Pacific. He died in the frozen wastes of the Arctic during the expedition. Louisa was a sister of Alfred`s eventual wife, Emily Sellwood.

The other member of the family who had already departed was Edward, who despite a valiant effort by the family to keep him at home, sadly had to be pronounced insane and confined to a private asylum. We will return to him later on.

High Beech had the advantage of being close to London, so Alfred was able to join up once again with his Cambridge friends and receive introductions to the London literary circle. It was high time he did so, for Lincolnshire is a remote place to make a name for oneself in the literary world, just as Yorkshire was to prove for the Brontë sisters.

Nevertheless, the wrench away from beloved Somersby was a painful one, and Alfred`s attraction to it comes out in constant references in his poetry. In 'Ode to Memory' he wrote:

"Come to the woods that belt the grey hill side,
The seven elms, the poplars four
That stand beside my father's door,
And chiefly from the brook that loves
To purl o'er matted cress and ribbed sand."

Nearby Stockwith Mill is reputedly the origin of his poem 'The Miller's Daughter'. There stood what Alfred described as the finest willow between Somersby and the sea. Of the Mill he wrote:

"I loved the brimming wave that swam
Thro' quiet meadows round the mill,
The sleepy pool above the dam,
The pool beneath it never still."

'The Brook' is likely to have been based on the stream that passes through Somersby. It eventually becomes the River Lymn and then the Steeping River as it nears the sea at Gibraltar Point. Alfred later became quite indignant when people tried to locate specific places in his poetry, claiming that they were not to be so defined.

The family's departure from Somersby in 1837 was also referred to in 'In Memoriam', his epic poem written in memory of Arthur Hallam:

"We leave the well-beloved place
Where first we gazed upon the sky;
The roofs that heard our earliest cry
Will shelter one of stranger race.

I turn to go; my feet are set
To leave the pleasant fields and farms;
They mix in one another's arms
To one pure image of regret."

Alfred appears never to have returned to Somersby after the family left for the south. The only member of the family who did return to visit childhood haunts, apart from Charles who settled in the county, was Mary.

Alfred's new circle of literary friends included Thackeray, Carlyle and Aubrey de Vere. Thomas Carlyle gave a vivid picture of his new young friend in a letter he wrote to a correspondent in the United States:

"A great stack of rough, dusky hair, bright, laughing hazel eyes, massive aquiline face, most massive yet most delicate, of sallow brown complexion, almost \Indian looking, clothes cynically loose, free and easy, smokes infinite tobacco. His voice is musical, metallic, fit for loud laughter and piercing wail, and all that may lie between; speech and speculation free and plenteous; I do not meet in these late decades such company over a pipe! We shall see what he will grow to."

Meanwhile, Alfred had hopes of marriage when the family was properly settled and he had the material means to support a family. The subject of his affections was now Emily Sellwood, whom he had first met at Somersby when Arthur Hallam was staying. They met again at Charles's wedding when Emily, the bride's sister, was a bridesmaid. In 1838 the couple became engaged, but Alfred was very conscious of the fact that his poetry was not producing enough income to support a family.

Another complication was the opposition of Emily's father Henry Sellwood, the Horncastle solicitor. He lived with his family in a handsome, three storey town house in the corner of Horncastle market place, which was demolished to make way for Woolworth's. He knew all about the melancholic side of the Tennyson character, for his daughter's marriage to Charles had not been a success, and Charles became more and more dependant on opiates. So what with one thing and another, the engagement drifted into a dormant state.

This was the most depressed time of Alfred's life. The family was unable to find a permanent home, moving on in 1840 to Tunbridge Wells and within a few months to Boxley in Kent. Worse was to follow the following year when the family lost all their capital, which had been invested in a scheme to carve furniture by machine. The scheme collapsed, and with it any prospects Alfred then had of marrying Emily.

His dress and outward appearance became even more wild and unkempt as depression took hold of him. He went off to Cheltenham as his father had done to try the cold water cure which was then so popular, and on his return threw himself into his writing with a newly found ardour.

And things started to pick up. When Sir Robert Peel had 'Ulysses' read to him by Monckton Miles he was so impressed that he granted Alfred a pension of £200 per annum from the Civil List, which relieved his financial difficulties. Then came the publication of 'The Princess' which was well received by the critics. He had thought constantly of Emily Sellwood through the thirteen years of their engagement, and now he decided to propose marriage to her. After some hesitation she accepted.

SUCCESS AT LAST

1850 was to prove a momentous year. In June, 'In Memoriam' was published anonymously, and had sold 60,000 copies by the end of the year. In the same month, Alfred and Emily were married at Shiplake by their friend Drummond Rawnsley. Emily was the kindest of souls, very religious and with a resolve of iron.

In the years that followed, it was her gentle yet determined guiding spirit that ruled the family. She provided for Alfred an idyllic family home and produced two sons, Hallam and Lionel, from whom he was inseparable. Alfred's own testament to his wife was: "The peace of God came into my life when I wedded her."

Just after their marriage, Aubrey de Vere wrote of his friend: "I have never before had so much pleasure in Alfred's society. He is far happier than I ever saw him before; and his 'wrath against the world' is proportionately mitigated."

The fortunes of 1850 received a further boost in November when Alfred was appointed Poet Laureate, on the death of William Wordsworth. At last he was receiving a comfortable living from his poetry, and house-hunting in earnest could begin. Their first choice, an isolated house near Horsham, was apparently haunted, and after sticking it for a few nights they abandoned their stoicism and left in haste, Alfred pushing Emily, who was already pregnant, along the Sussex lanes in a bath chair.

Their second abode, Chapel House in Twickenham, had the advantages of London literary society, but their first son was stillborn there and this blighted it because of those sad memories. Hallam was also born there, but a move was decided upon to a house without tragedy lurking in an upstairs bedroom.

And so on a misty November day in 1853 the family crossed the Solent and arrived at Farringford, near Freshwater, on the rocky western extremity of the Isle of Wight. Although Emily's maids burst into tears when they first gazed at the solitude of the place, Emily and Alfred loved it, for it had downs to walk on, chalk cliffs rising vertically from the English Channel, a perpetual crescendo from the seagulls and the peace that Alfred required for his poetry.

The following spring Lionel was born, and later in the year 'The Charge of the Light Brigade' was published in 'The Examiner'. Lincolnshire must have seemed a long way away both in distance and in association, but Alfred showed his affectionate memories for the county of his birth when he published 'Maud' and other poems in 1855.

"Birds in the high hall garden" is a direct reference to Harrington Hall, and the poem goes on to recall his infatuation with Rosa Baring, almost 30 years earlier:

> "Where was Maud? In our wood;
>   And I, who else, was with her,
> Gathering woodland lilies
>   Myriads blown together.
>
> Birds in our wood sang
>   Ringing thro' the valleys,
> Maud is here, here, here
>   In among the lilies."

The poem was badly received by the critics but Alfred loved it, and would recite it to anyone who would listen, including his two young sons whom he strapped to his back as he paced the downs.

No doubt Queen Victoria herself read it, who invited Alfred to visit her at Osborne House in 1862. They got on really well together, and Prince Albert was equally enthusiastic about the regal choice of Poet Laureate. By now Alfred had friends in high places apart from royal patronage, for Gladstone, Robert Browning and Edward Lear were also ardent admirers. Apart from his nonsense verse, the latter was fast achieving a reputation as a talented artist.

And so Alfred Tennyson came to be regarded as one of the most eminent figures of his generation. He was fast becoming very well off from his writing, and was able to purchase Aldworth, a summer residence rather closer to the metropolis, near Haslemere.

He continued to write verse into old age, for he was 70 when he wrote that finest of all sea ballads, 'The Revenge', and 80 when he produced

'Crossing the Bar'. This was partly written on the ferry which chugs across from Yarmouth on the Isle of Wight to Lymington on the mainland.

The final accolade of national admiration arrived in 1883 when he was knighted Baron Tennyson of Aldworth and Freshwater, and it was at Aldworth that he died in 1892 at the age of 83. He was buried in Westminster Abbey alongside his contemporary, Robert Browning.

His mastery as a poet is well summed up by Sidgwick, who wrote: "He has that inborn instinct for the subtle power of language and for musical sound; that feeling for beauty in phrase and thought, and that perfection of form which, taken all together, we call poetry."

Those of us who have spent so many happy hours engrossed in his poems and enraptured by his romantic, lyrical stories will add a hearty and spontaneous "Hear! Hear!"

EDWARD AND SEPTIMUS

To complete the family picture, mention must be made of Alfred's younger brothers Edward and Septimus. Both suffered acutely from the traits of melancholia and unquiet minds that ran in the family. Edward was the sixth surviving child of the family and the fourth son, four years younger than Alfred. He did not attend the Grammar School at Louth until he was fourteen, and even then it is doubtful whether he survived his first term.

Two years later, George Clayton wrote to his father about a proposed visit to Tealby, a letter quoted by Christopher Sturman in 'Lincolnshire People and Places':

"I shall bring Edward with me, as you have been so good as to interest yourself in his behalf. At home he will be quite ruined, and he is beginning to be what you call chippy and unmanageable... He must be governed and know what it is to have a master. He is already running restive and what am I to expect from a boy who has been at home nearly a year upon the plea of ill health, and encouraged as he is. He will stay at home all his life and be ignorant and impudent. Upon this subject, however, I shall converse with you, and you have shown yourself so much the friend of my family that I will most willingly and confidentially trust to you, as to what is to be done with Edward, a very awkward and unlicked fellow who fancies himself to be a superior genius and who scarcely knows that two and two makes four."

A year later Edward himself showed the frustrations of being a youth of 17 confined to the house in remote Somersby without any prospects, when he wrote to his grandfather a plea for help. His father was in Italy at the time, and his three older brothers up at Cambridge:

"I should be exceedingly obliged to you if you would place me in some profession. I am quite certain a farmer would be the most suitable for my health as well as my choice, since a life of activity would enable me to shake off all lassitude and despondency which at present I labour under from my want of employment. If some step is not immediately taken in my favour, I must inevitably resign all pretensions to any business, otherwise I must be an annuitant. My brothers all agree in saying that I ought to be put out to something. What do you think I should do?"

Nothing very concrete seems to have resulted from this plea, for a year later in 1831 it was the turn of Uncle Charles to write to old George Tennyson at Tealby about his grandson. This was shortly after the death of Edward's father, George Clayton. Charles wrote as follows:

"Edward is understood to be unfit for any thrift – and I fear must remain at home - but Alfred says that he really fears that his mind will at length so prey upon itself, that he cannot answer for consequencies. It is difficult to devise anything for him as employment with a real object. Alfred says he should if possible go from home and be amused. He has often fancied he should like to be a farmer – but as farming requires as much wit as calling – I do not think we can look at that matter seriously. If Eliza (Edward's mother) should finally move to Buckden, then he might get into some variety of life which might relieve his mind – but I fear that if he were sent from home to mix with the world by himself – he would become unhappy from another source as he would find himself unequal to his companions and perhaps be exposed to ridicule which his sensitive mind could not endure. Poor fellow! I feel for him and will endeavour as far as I can to soften his existence for him – but that existence never, I fear, can be a happy one."

The letter reflects highly on Uncle Charles, showing a lot of genuine compassion. But he was right. Edward's existence was never a happy one, and by 1832 it was decided that there was nothing for it but to consign Edward to a private mental asylum at Acomb, near York. This was run by Mr. H.B. Hodgson, son of a former vicar of Tealby. The whole process was rather a pitiful charade, for Edward was told that his position there would be as an assistant to Mr. Hodgson, not an inmate. Edward's mother wrote to Uncle Charles about the arrangements in November 1832:

"The plan about to be adopted with respect to poor Edward, appears to me as far as I can judge to be a desirable one, and I feel obliged to you for wishing to place him under the care of a humane person who will use him kindly, as I am convinced a contrary treatment would only aggravate his disorder. He weeps bitterly sometimes, and says his mind is so unnotched he is scarcely able to endure his existence and requires encouragement rather than severity. Perhaps you would be so good as to inform me by what Conveyance Mr. Tennyson wishes Edward to be sent to York, who is to accompany him and also to let me know the Gentleman's address under whose care he is to be placed."

As was the custom with Victorian families, the matter was hushed up, and as far as the neighbourhood was concerned Edward had gone off to study medicine. In due course it was implied that he had died. But Edward was not completely forgotten by his family. Grandfather George left him £3,000 in his will, and his brother Charles visited him from time to time. It is also known that Alfred spent a night in York in 1852, presumably to visit his younger brother.

One feels so sorry for Edward, whose condition was probably not only due to the melancholic tendencies of the Tennysons. The traumas of the early years at Somersby Rectory must have played some part in his gradual derangement, and so he became a lonely and forsaken figure who drifted into old age in his institutional isolation. He died only two years before Alfred, at the age of 77.

Only a year or two after Edward had been packed off to York, the family had cause to worry about Septimus, the eighth surviving child. Alfred wrote to his Uncle Charles in 1834, fearing that his mind would become as deranged as Edward's unless he could be found some active line of fulfilment well away from the memories of Somersby.

"He is subject to fits of the most gloomy despondency accompanied by tears," wrote Alfred, "or rather, he spends whole days in this manner, complaining that he is neglected by all his relations, and blindly resigning himself to every morbid influence."

Eventually he was sent to be an apprentice to the family physician, Dr. Boucefield of Horncastle, but this lasted no more than a year. He was in and out of mental asylums as a voluntary patient, and eventually settled with his mother in London. Even the long-suffering Elizabeth found it hard to cope with him, probably because of what his aunt referred to as "his unfortunate habit" – presumably drugs. Septimus then took lodgings not far away, and so life meandered on until his death at the age of 51.

Both Edward and Septimus wrote verse, some of Edward`s in particular being rather good. His 'Sonnet on Holbeck' has considerable charm, Holbeck being an estate at Ashby Puerorum, about two miles from Somersby.

FOOTNOTE

Alfred`s grandson, The Hon. Lionel Tennyson, became a notable cricketer, playing for England on nine occasions between 1913 and 1921 and captaining Hampshire. In this latter capacity he featured in one of the most remarkable matches ever played in the County Championship.

Hampshire was playing Warwickshire in June 1922 at Edgbaston. The hosts scored 223 and then, on a placid enough wicket, skittled Hampshire out for 15 in less than nine overs. This was all on the first day, and in the pavilion after play the home captain, Freddie Gough-Calthorpe, suggested that the amateurs in the match should play golf as soon as the game was over the next morning.

This remark really roused Tennyson, as did a postcard received in the Hampshire dressing-room on the following morning suggesting that his team should take up painting spots on rocking horses. He placed a handsome bet on Hampshire winning the match at astronomical odds, then probably wished he hadn`t when Hampshire following on were 274 for eight wickets, and only 69 ahead. At this point Hampshire`s No. 10 batsman, Walter Livsey, proceeded to score a century – all the more remarkable as this innings apart, he only scored a further 181 runs in the entire season.

Hampshire amassed 521, bowled Warwickshire out for 158 and so won the game by 155 runs. Never has there been such a remarkable recovery in the history of the Championship, and never, in all probability, did Lionel Tennyson win a bet again at such outrageous odds. His grandfather, who always supported the underdog, would have delighted in the occasion.

THE TENNYSON VILLAGES

HARRINGTON

If the traveller from Horncastle turns left off the busy A158 road at Hagworthingham, and leaves the steady stream of traffic heading for the fish and chips and sandy delights of Skegness, he or she will be in the lanes of the southern Wolds. It is of course a cliché to say that this countryside is like England was 50 years ago, but in the Tennyson villages of Harrington, Somersby and Bag Enderby it really is true.

Because of the Tennyson connection there will be a few visitors around in the height of summer, but for nine months in the year the villages enjoy the tranquility of time immemorial. None of the lanes ever become pretentious enough to be classed as roads, there are no shops, hotels, garden centres, garages or such like, and no pub closer than Tetford. But the visitor can obtain tea in lovely surroundings at Stockwith Mill.

Harrington announces itself almost a mile before one gets to it in every direction, so the unsuspecting traveller expects something rather special. And so it is, but not perhaps in the way the traveller expects, for it is hardly a village at all. It consists of Harrington Hall, St. Mary's Church, the old rectory next door, a farm and a modern house.

There are maybe ten other houses scattered about away from the centre of the village, but there are only 34 names on the Register of Electors, so perhaps the total population may consist of around 50. In 1841 the village had 107 people in it, 114 in 1851, 123 in 1881, 101 in 1891 and 102 in 1901, so unlike many of the villages in these parts it did not suffer in the agricultural recession of the 19th century. This was probably due to the Hall, which would have employed most of the population.

To appreciate Harrington Hall fully, it should first be viewed on foot, walking along the lane from Stockwith Mill. With the afternoon sun illuminating the red brick west front, and the central porch breaking the long line of symmetrical windows by rising the entire height of the building, it looks from the lane like one of the fine old country seats of Lincolnshire. In fact it is not, for it was burnt down in 1991.

But the present owners have meticulously rebuilt it, sticking as far as possible to its original design, apart from practical improvements such as siting the kitchen in a more convenient location so that dinner does not arrive stone cold from its travels through the nether regions. The house is not open to the public, although the gardens are accessible at certain advertised times.

Harrington is an idyllic spot, nestling under the downs where fields, streams and woods all come together in a gentle alliance between nature and man. There would have been more going on there in 1851, when John Gant kept a shop in the village, and William Daubney, one of the five farmers, ran the post office.

The Hall at that time was owned by The Rev'd. H.J. Ingilby, the patron of the living, but he did not live in it. That honour was bestowed upon his gamekeeper, Henry Brooks, who could have changed his bedroom almost every day of the month if he felt like it.

In 1881 the two leading farmers, John Davey and John Baumber employed almost everyone living in the village either at the Hall or. John Davey at Rectory Farm employed thirteen men and four boys in his fields. He and his wife had six children, so a governess, a nurse and a general domestic complemented the household. John Baumber had a servant, a nurse, a groom and seven men to help him around the farm.

Meaburn Staniland, a retired military man, owned the Hall at that time. He lived there along with his elder son James, a clergyman without a living, his second son Alfred who was an Oxford undergraduate and his daughter Matilda. To cater for every need they employed a cook, three housemaids, a kitchen maid, a nurse and a footman.

The rector of Harrington and Brinkhill then was Robert Wentworth Cracroft, a widower aged 54, who employed a housekeeper, a maid, a cook and a 14-year-old page. He was a native of the place, for he was the youngest son of Robert Cracroft and his wife Augusta, daughter of Sir John Ingilby of Ripley Castle, Yorkshire.

He clearly enjoyed living among the woods and fields beneath the gently sloping hills, with the pheasants far more numerous than his parishoners, for he held the living for 54 years. There is still a picture of him in the vestry of the church, a bald, scholarly, kindly-looking man with a neatly trimmed beard, studying a book at an intricately carved table. His flock clearly valued their incumbent, for underneath his memorial in the church are the words: "He was ever a faithful friend and counsellor to his parishoners and neighbours, by whom he was beloved and respected."

The 1881 census lists the Harrington residents as agricultural labourers, dairymaid, greengrocer, wheelwright, under-gardener, groom, shepherd, coachman and gamekeeper. Some of them probably never went further than Spilsby, Louth and Horncastle in their entire lives, and lie at peace in the churchyard.

The church of St. Mary is approached from the road by a path which winds between the holly bushes to emerge into a clearing of sheltered tranquility. In November the wind murmurs in the tree-tops, the bare twigs suspend raindrops like premature Christmas decorations, and irreverent moles have excavated their sodden heaps between the graves. The rain drips relentlessly on the decaying leaves and the nettles hug the gravestones as if in relief at escaping the scythes of summer.

But there is nothing gloomy about this spot, bordered by the tall brick wall of Harrington Hall, the woods and the old rectory garden. It is an immortal place, the atmosphere perhaps heightened by the gravestones, the same yesterday, today and forever. One feels that the spirits buried here have no need to tramp abroad in anguish, come Hallowe'en.

Some of the larger gravestones are protected by iron railings as if to ward off the wolves from the woods, or as a gesture of privacy from those not so well endowed with this world's goods when they tramped the lanes of the village. A tall conifer rises king of the clearing, even higher than the church tower.

In the middle of the clearing stands the grey stone church, its old tower guarded by the gargoyle of a lion, gazing down as if to inspect whether the members of the early morning congregation have brushed their hair. The tower arch is medieval, and the belfry has wide open arches to allow the bells to summons the villagers from their beds.

Although the church was heavily restored in 1855 – 56 by Robert Cracroft, the interior is a delight. Above the chancel arch there is a miniature lantern or Sanctus bellcote. There is some fine tracery in the Decorated style, with foliage and headstops abounding. The octagonal font dates from the 15th century, approached by an old stone step for rectors who are not over-endowed with inches. Each of the sides of the font is adorned by a shield, held up by a figure, and these are the coats of arms of the Copeldikes who donated the font so long ago.

Several of the impressive memorials in the church commemorate members of the Copeldike family, although the grandest of all belongs to Sir John Harrington and dates from around 1300. He lies in a crevice beside the pulpit, his shield at the ready to fend off any stinging words from a pacifist preacher. One foot is placed disdainfully over a rather meek lion, crouching in abeyance.

Another fine tomb in the chancel commemorates Margaret Copuldyk and dates from 1480. She has an elaborate stone canopy above her to keep away the spiders. Originally she lay beside her husband, but he has disappeared with the ages. Her tomb is constructed from Purbeck marble, brought all the way from Dorset by a 15th century haulier.

Beneath the tower there is a tombchest of black stone with three shields in roundels. This bears an inscription to Sir John Copeldyke dated 1552, while his wife Ann and son rest in a canopied tomb against the back wall, erected in 1585. Both are kneeling at desks. In 1599 an alabaster tomb forms the memorial to Francis Copeldyke – the fourth variation in spelling – and his wife Elizabeth, who is adorned in a farthingale. Kneeling behind them are their two children, who sadly died when still young.

But the line did not die out with them, for in 1658 appeared a stone to Francis's nephew Thomas, who was clearly a popular figure around the village for his epitaph reads: "Of ancient stock, here lies the last and best."

Robert Cracroft has been criticised in some quarters for his radical restoration of the church in 1855 – 56, at a cost of £1,000, but it was probably a necessity. Many village churches in the first half of the 19th century were close to ruinous, and their decay flagged the spirits of both clergy and congregations. Reynolds Hole, who spent 68 years of his life at the Manor House at Caunton, near Newark, progressively as schoolboy, undergraduate, curate, vicar and squire, describes in his 'Memories' his early experiences of churchgoing at Caunton:

"Our curate, who lived five miles away, rode over for one dreary service on the Sunday, dined, and we saw him no more during the week. He was much occupied in the pursuit of the fox, which, it is charitable to suppose, he mistook for a wolf, and like a good shepherd was anxious to destroy. The service was literally a duet between the parson and the clerk, except when old John Manners, the bricklayer, gave the keynote for the hymn from his bassoon, a sound which might have been uttered by an elephant in distress, and we sang:

> 'O turn my pi... O turn my pi... O turn my pious soul to Thee',

or when the curate suddenly emerged from his surplice, which he placed on the side of his reading-pew, and appearing in his academical gown, went up the 'three-decker' to preach. The altar was represented by a small, rickety, deal table, with a scanty covering of faded and patched green baize, on which were placed the overcoat, hat and riding-whip of the officiating minister, who made a vestry within the sacrarium, and sitting there in a huge surplice, had a conversation with the sexton before the service began, and looked as though he were about to have his hair cut. The font was filled with coffin ropes, tinderboxes and brimstone matches, candle ends, etc. It was never used for baptism. Zebah and Zalmunna would not have countenanced such an unseemly interruption of the service. Sparrows twittered and bats floated beneath the rotten surface of the roof, while beetles and moths, and all manner of flies, found happy homes below. The damp walls represented in fresco 'a green and yellow melancholy', which had a depressing influence on the spirit, and the darkest and most dismal building in the parish was that called the House of God."

Such conditions could be found in many a village church, and although much that was ancient would have been destroyed by Cracroft during his restoration, we must at least give him some credit for the beauty of St. Mary's today. Ancient and modern blend harmoniously together. Candles still provide light at the pulpit and candle-holders remain on the organ, although the venerable instrument is now blessed with electricity.

A 20th century benefactor has added the attractive east window, showing the Blessed Virgin Mary, flanked by St. Ursula and St. Francis, and embroiderers in recent years have provided the kneelers which depict everything from the Woodman`s Cottage on the road to Bag Enderby to the inevitable pheasants.

HARRINGTON HALL

Next door to the church stands Harrington Hall, resplendent in a small park, a veritable Phoenix risen from the ashes of that tragic night in November 1991 when a blowtorch being used for burning off old paintwork reaped such havoc in the strong winds. But the present owners have rebuilt it with a loving care for detail, so that it stands today as magnificent as ever.

The original early Tudor house would have been a sandstone building of two storeys, the upper one probably constructed of timber and plaster, with mullioned windows symmetrically placed. A brick porch, built in Henry VIII's time, adorned the west front, ending in a stepped gable above which was a high pitched roof and dormer windows. The east court probably had three projecting gables with shallow courts in between them.

Platforms suggesting an even earlier building have been found in the park. On the far side of the lane leading to Hagworthingham there is a copse which contains the remains of what appears to have been a moat. During alterations in the early part of the 20th century, the digging of a drain on the churchyard side of the Hall uncovered a number of human remains in a grave extending underneath a building immediately to the north of the Hall. The remains were charred, suggesting that the victims were caught in a fire and burnt to death.

Another possibility is that they were victims of the Black Death, which was rampant in these parts. The burning could be accounted for by lime or some other medieval ingredient which acted as a cleansing agent. Up to recent times, gravediggers were instructed to wear protective clothing and gloves as a precautionary measure against malign matter which still might lurk in the soil.

The building under which the communal grave was found, now demolished, was of timber grain infilled with brick, and was probably built of materials from the Tudor main house, as the timbers show signs of having been used before. When the doorposts were taken up, one was found to stand upon a jamb dated 1535.

The bricks for the Tudor Harrington Hall were probably made from the nearest source of clay, which is the valley behind the Woodman's Cottage. The clay would have been burnt in kilns near the house, with estate timber being used as fuel. In those days, two men could make 48,000 bricks at one firing, at a cost of six shillings per thousand.

Part of the long west frontage was Elizabethan, and the lower part of the porch retained its early brickwork until the fire. The house belonged to the Copeldikes until 1658, when it passed to the Amcotts on the death of Thomas Copeldike. Vincent Amcotts embarked on an extensive rebuilding of the house from 1673 – 78, probably using as his architect William Catlyn of Hull, who was building Brigg Grammar School at the same time. Vincent Amcotts was a trustee of the school, so the two men would have known eachother.

The rebuilt Charles II house was rectangular, with a frontage extending to 125 feet. It was built of brick on a sandstone plinth, and the porch effectively broke up the length of the west front by again rising the entire height of the building. The restorers left in position a hexagonal pier about 26 feet high which shows that the Tudor house was similar in height, as indeed is the Hall of today. The pier had to be removed during repairs early in the 20th century, but the base remains.

The interior floor of the building was raised in the 1678 restoration because a layer of tiles was found about a foot below the surface. Tudor work also exists in the cellar under the north end of the building, which was found to contain a slab, presumably from the church and possibly a Copeldike memorial.

The renovated house contained an impressive entrance hall, featuring a wide elliptical arch with a span of about 17 feet. From it rose a superb staircase, made from very dark oak and heavily panelled, approached through arcaded and fanlighted doors. The present staircase is equally impressive, made after the fire by craftsmen from Stamford.

The bedrooms were all panelled, with repeating pilasters and cornices from the floor below. Above them were ten attics, placed between the enormous beams which formed the roof. When this was restored early in the 20th century, the 300-year-old Westmoreland slates were found to be in excellent condition, so they were simply cleaned and replaced.

One of the highlights of the Charles II house was the oak room, which was panelled from floor to ceiling. About three-quarters of the walls were panelled with linen-pattern work, but the top quarter, which formed a kind of frieze below the ceiling, was adorned with grotesque carvings. Each panel featured some weird creature, beautifully carved as a labour of real love. They did escape the fire, and are now part of the Burrell collection in Glasgow.

J.J. Hissey refers to them in his book 'Over Fen and Wold', published in 1898, and probably had sleepless nights for the rest of the month. "Some of the designs, indeed, were so outrageous as to suggest the work of a craftsman fresh from Bedlam," he wrote. "One could hardly, in the most romantically poetic mood, have given (the creations) credit for existing in this or any other planet where things might be ordered differently; they are all, or nearly all, distinctly impossible. On one of these panels is shown a creature with the head and neck of a swan, the body of a fish (from which body proceeded scaled wings of the prehistoric reptile kind) and a spreading feathered tail somewhat like a peacock's; the creature had one human foot and one claw! – a very nightmare in carving, and a bad nightmare to boot! Another nondescript animal, leading to a dragon, was provided with two heads, one in the usual place, and one in the tail with a big eye, each head regarding the other wonderingly. Another creature looked for all the world like a gigantic mouse with a long curling tail, but his head was that of a man." It would seem that the 17th century had the same fascination for Dungeons and Dragons as we do today.

The famous weathervane dated 1678 was a victim of the fire, but has been replaced by a handsome replica. The sundial bearing the Amcotts coat of arms over the doorway, dated three years later, did survive the fire, but was found to be a reproduction anyway for reasons explained later. The terrace was constructed from the rubble of the old Tudor house in the 1678 restoration, and is a fine vantage point from which to view the park and the gently sweeping countryside to the west.

The lay-out of the grounds was the work of an 18th century landscape gardener, and included the fine walled garden immediately behind the house, and behind that a wood with the remains of an oblong canal and a lime avenue. The walls of the walled garden date from Henry VII's time. The shape is ideal for a bowling green and it is likely that Tudor gentlemen amused themselves in the summer heat by copying the antics of Sir Francis Drake.

The later Amcotts were close friends of George Clayton Tennyson and Elizabeth, so Alfred would have known the house and grounds intimately. As stated earlier, the garden is reputed to have been the origin of his famous line "Come into the garden, Maud" while the rooks, which are still very much in evidence, were the inspiration for the verse:

> "Birds in the high Hall garden
> When twilight was fading,
> Maud, Maud, Maud, Maud,
> They were crying and calling."

The Amcotts were descendants of the Copeldikes, and in turn the ownership of the Hall passed from the Amcotts to the Ingilbys, who were relatives of theirs by marriage. From 1814 Harrington was owned by Robert Cracroft, who acquired it by his marriage to Augusta Amcotts Ingilby, the second daughter of Sir John Ingilby of Kettlethorpe Park, Lincolnshire, and Ripley Castle, Yorkshire. In 1854 the couple added the additional surname of Amcotts when Augusta succeeded to the Kettlethorpe estate on the death of her brother, Sir William Amcotts Ingilby.

Robert and Augusta lived at Harrington until the mid 1820's by which time Cracroft's father had died and the main family estate at Hackthorn, north of Lincoln, was available. They moved there, and leased out Harrington. Their second daughter was also called Augusta. In 1840 she married The Rev'd Charles Jarvis of Doddington, and their third son Robert Wentworth, born in 1826, was to become rector of Harrington and Brinkhill for 54 years.

The second tenant at Harrington was Arthur Eden from Wimbledon, who moved there with his wife Frances (widow of William Baring, M.P.) and his step-daughters Fanny, Georgiana and Rosa Baring. It was, of course, Rosa who so infatuated Alfred in the romance referred to in the Tennyson chapters.

Eden's tenancy at Harrington is described in fascinating detail by Christopher Sturman in his paper 'Arthur Eden and Harrington Hall', from which the following details are taken. Eden moved to Harrington in March 1831 and paid an annual rent of £150 for the furnished house "with the yards and gardens thereunto belonging... also the Park with several pieces or parcels of land... within the Park paling containing 32 acres... also the manors... of Harrington, Brinkhill and Hagworthingham... with full liberty to hunt, course, shoot and sport over and upon the lands of... Robert Cracroft and Augusta his wife in Harrington, Brinkhill and Hagworthingham."

Arthur Eden was to remain the tenant of Harrington until October 1839 when he and his wife returned to London. The day after his departure he wrote to his brother-in-law Lord Brougham stating, "It went to my heart to leave Harrington – the family leave it today." They had enjoyed the social life of the area as well as the sport, frequently dining with the Rawnsleys at Halton Holegate, the Massingberds of Ormsby, the Cholmeleys from Wainfleet, the Yorkes at Walmsgate and so on. They often attended balls at Lincoln and Horncastle, where Tennysons, Rawnsleys and Fytches were generally of the company, along with Robert Shafto who was to marry Rosa in 1838.

Lord Brougham spent the summer of 1836 convalescing at Harrington, and his wife gave her considered opinion of the house in her diary: "A curious fine old house, but dull and retired beyond all precedent – the gardens ugly bad and rough – or rather no walks." She clearly had failed to bring her wellington boots with her.

Another frequent visitor to Harrington at this time was The Rev'd. F.C. Massingberd, rector of Ormsby-cum-Ketsby. He was not entirely welcome, judging by Mrs. Eden's letter to her brother Lord Brougham, written in 1834: "You were when here asking about my girls and their amusements, Fanny and her Mouldy as we call him, the Massingberd who lives at the parsonage near, whom we feared she had taken a fancy to, but she has seen him fortunately so few times that I think she must give up all hope now."

The courtship did not therefore sound too promising, especially as Massingberd's mother was even more antagonistic, and the clergyman clearly found the Eden household too much infested with temptations of the devil for his Puritanical taste. He disapproved of the gentlemen playing cards ("record now my solemn protest against myself if I ever permit it at my house") and found the family, including his fiancé, irreligious.

But his proposal was made nevertheless, and it seems strange that the lively Fanny accepted it. But she did, and just before the marriage in 1839, when the Edens had moved back to London, Massingberd visited the family again, only to record: "No reference to God! No prayers in family! No suggestion of affection at losing her!" One hopes the family was blissfully happy together, despite the inevitable tensions when the Mothers-in-law came to stay!

The next tenant of Harrington Hall was The Rev'd. John Thomas Maine, who was married to Robert Cracroft's niece, Eliza. He became both rector and squire of Harrington in 1839, the plan being that he would hold the living until Cracroft's third son Robert Wentworth became ordained, whereupon he would inherit the family living. He had his own rectory built in 1851 on the other side of the church from the Hall, and so tenants continued to be installed at Harrington.

At one time in the mid 19th century the occupant was Henry Brooks, the gamekeeper, and another tenant was Thomas Shaw Hillier, Master of the Southwold Hunt. We have already seen that at the time of the 1881 census Maeburn Staniland, M.P. for Boston, was in residence. He was a tenant there for 40 years. His son had an inventory made, showing that they produced their own wine and brewed their own beer on the premises.

By the time J.J. Hissey visited the Hall in the late 1890's he found it tenantless and empty, beset by a sadly forsaken look. He obtained the keys from Robert Cracroft at the rectory and wrote of his visit in 'Over Fen and Wold':

"The deserted Hall was gloomy and ghost-like, with dismal, if large, bed chambers leading one into the other in an uncomfortable sort of way, and huge cupboards like little windowless rooms, and rambling passages – a house that had manifestly been altered from time to time with much confusion to its geography. A sense of mystery hung over all, and suggested to us that the place must be haunted."

Early in the 20th century the tenant was Edward Preston Rawnsley, another Master of the Southwold Hunt. He held this office for 40 years and made it a full time occupation, for he hunted six days a week until he was 70. In the 1920's, when Major Tom Jessop was the owner, the Hall faced a real threat of demolition, but a change of heart found it put up for auction in various lots in 1927.

On the morning of the auction Major W.H. Rawnsley, a cousin of the master of the hunt, bought the Hall for £1,000. But it was so close to the start of the auction when he put his signature to the title deeds that this had to go ahead, nonetheless. The staircase had already been sold, so Rawnsley had to trace down the purchaser and buy it back. The sundial over the porch had also already been under the hammer, and as the purchaser would not relinquish it, Rawnsley was forced to make do with a reproduction.

Rawnsley later sold Harrington to Holliday Hartley for £1,500, a condition of the sale being that if he in turn ever sold it on, he would give first option of purchase either to the National Trust or to the Rawnsley family. During the Second World War Harrington was used to house Dr. Barnado evacuees from Sheffield.

Eventually in 1950 it was purchased by Commander Sir John and Lady Maitland, who already owned the nearby Somersby estate. Sir John was a naval gunnery officer who later became M.P. for Horncastle. The present owners, Mr. And Mrs. David Price, suffered the traumas of the fire, but have resurrected their home to stand once again with the great houses of Lincolnshire.

On the other side of the church from the Hall stands the old rectory in its well wooded garden. This is an interesting house to squint at through the trees, and looks older than it is. It was built in 1851 and was probably designed by S.S. Teulon, an architect of some repute who was also responsible for the restoration of the church. The house looks ideal as the setting for an Alfred Hitchcock thriller, but is probably a tranquil abode with the aura of scholarly and saintly incumbents lurking in its passages.

All the other mud and stud cottages which used to compose Harrington have disappeared with the winter gales apart from one, the old

Woodman's Cottage on the lane to Bag Enderby. This has been extended, restored and rethatched, the roof sweeping down so low on the eastern side that a child of eight would have to bend to hide underneath it. The woodman of former years certainly attended to his replanting, for the trees engulf it in a cocoon of greenery.

THE OLD RECTORY AT SOMERSBY

BAG ENDERBY

It is easy to Miss Bag Enderby altogether unless you watch out for the sign on the lane which winds along from Harrington to Somersby. But just off the lane stands the church, and clustered round it are the nine houses and cottages, the homes of the 18 souls who comprise its total population today.

Once again the church is built of greensand, the rock which underlies the chalk in these parts. It changes colour like a chameleon, depending upon what kind of day it is. In the sun the stones gleam a mellow orange, but when the winter drizzle comes they turn to a mouldy dark green or grey.

It is a lovely little church, dedicated to St. Margaret, where services are normally held once a month. There must be a temptation from the ecclesiastical authorities to close churches like this, for it is an annual struggle to meet the diocesan quota. Indeed, it is a sad fact that churches normally feature among the desirable residential properties in the estate agents' windows in Horncastle and Louth. With dwindling congregations it is so easy to follow the cost efficiency route of British Rail under Beecham or the high street banks and call it a day.

But this brave little church has survived so much through the centuries, and it would be abhorrent to imagine it ever being deconsecrated, as has been the fate of the church at Driby. Fortunately, the South Ormsby group of parishes is at present determined to retain it as one of its nine churches, all served by one over-worked parish priest.

Alfred Tennyson would have known this church well as a boy and a young man, for he lived less than a mile away and his father was the rector here as well as at neighbouring Somersby. Much of what we see today would have been familiar to him. The rough, greenstone blocks of the tower are just the same, with four gargoyles hanging out into space, as if defying the great discovery of Isaac Newton.

He would have passed no doubt reluctantly from the sun into the moss-covered porch as a boy, some 180 years ago, and imagined during his father's sermon the gruesome fate of the Saxon whose shield boss is still attached to the massive oak door. The first thing to strike the visitor inside is the light, which streams in through the unusually wide, plain glass windows.

It is a simple, well loved little church, with bare flagstones, whitewashed walls and a beautifully carved little pulpit, where the Bible is illuminated by candles. In many respects it is a time-warp of the past history of the hamlet. There are brasses to commemorate Thomas and Agnes Enderby who lived here in 1390, and Albinus de Enderby who left money for the building of the tower in 1407.

Near the door stands a very fine old Perpendicular font, perched on two broken tombstones. Every side has its own Biblical carving, one depicting the Virgin Mary with the dead body of Christ. There is also David with a viol, a running deer turning to lick from its back the tree of life and a shield with the instruments of the Passion.

If one looks carefully at the segmental arches of the windows, fragments of medieval glass are visible. These came from Crowland Abbey, south of Spalding, whose arms are depicted along with knives and scourges from the Abbey. It used to be a strange custom to give little knives to anyone coming to Crowland on St. Bartholomew's Day, and one wonders how the glass found its way over 40 miles of Lincolnshire field and fen to end up here.

The vestry extends upwards into the tower, where there used to be a very fine peal of bells. At least one remains, for an ancient rope, worn smooth with age, dangles down from a considerable height. No doubt the youthful Tennyson pulled it with zest, whenever he was allowed to. One of his poems refers to Christmas bells in these villages:

> "The time draws near the birth of Christ,
> The moon is hid; the night is still;
> The Christmas bells from hill to hill
> Answer each other in the mist.
>
> Four voices of four hamlets round,
> From far and near; on mead and moor;
> Swell out and fail, as if a door
> Were shut between me and the sound."

A monument on the north wall of the chancel of a man in armour and his wife kneeling at a desk, accompanied by their two sons and two daughters, commemorates Andrew Gadney and his wife Dorothy, who died in 1591. Most of the other tablets are in memory of the Burton family. William Langhorne Burton died in 1739 and is commemorated along with his wife Mary. Over a century later William Burton Burton and his wife Ann have their memorial.

By the year 1856 we find that most of the land in the parish was owned by The Rev'd. Langhorne Burton, who resided at Somersby Rectory. He was lord of the manor, patron and rector of both Bag Enderby and Somersby. There were three shopkeepers in the village, which then had a population of 116. One of them, Thomas Bark, was also a carrier, paying frequent visits to Horncastle, Spilsby and Louth, and no doubt his cart was equipped for humans as well as potatoes, hay and vegetables.

George Pape, another of the shopkeepers, was a shoemaker, while Allison Clarke combined the duties of village tailor with parish clerk. There was also a blacksmith called John Hewson resident in the village, and three independent farmers.

25 years later, in the 1881 census, the population had dwindled to 71, residing in a mere thirteen houses. The most influential person in the village was now Alfred Davey, who lived at Old Hall with his wife Mary, two sons and five daughters. He employed six men and a boy on the farm, and not surprisingly a governess, two domestic servants and a groom.
The blacksmith's forge had passed into the hands of John Hackney, whose five sons and three daughters no doubt did their share of courting in the fields with the Davey offspring. He employed an 18-year-old apprentice, George Bell. There was still a blacksmith and his forge in the village in 1937. Also resident in the village in 1881 was a curate, The Rev'd. Harry Greenwood, along with his wife Harriet and their two infants. The couple employed a nursemaid and a domestic servant for the nappies.

It is to be hoped that Harry Greenwood kept his sermons short or his congregation might have been in danger of hypothermia, for 30 years later the church was described as being in a very ruinous state. In 1956

– 58 it was subjected to a major restoration, but despite the various whims and tastes of restorers over the centuries, the chancel screen has been left intact. Part of it dates from the 15th century, and it is indeed a fine addition to this simple but delightful little church.

Out in the churchyard is an old cross, desecrated by the Roundheads after their victory over the Royalists at the Battle of Winceby in 1643. Only the original base remains today, guarded by colonies of cawing rooks from the treetops. To the south-west they cast covetous looks at the winter wheat in the gently sloping valley with its streams and copses, interspersed by outlying farmhouses.

Opposite the church is Ferndale Manor, once the old rectory, showing its status by the family coat of arms on the gates. It is a glorious mixture of fine old mellow brick, all the roofs of the various wings at different levels and the chimneys seemingly competing with one another as to which can reach the highest.

Bag Enderby Hall, now a farmhouse, has endured a fire, but parts of it date from the 17th century. Another house nearby, Ivy House Farm, is also worth a peep. This was originally built of the traditional mud and stud construction as a single storey house with a thatched roof and a central chimney-stack, but it has now been restored rather attractively.

On the green, where the Bag Enderby lane leaves the road from Harrington, is the shell of an old wytch elm of enormous girth, under whose boughs John Wesley is reputed to have preached. The trunk of the old tree decayed to such an extent that children used to play in it, and the Tennyson children built a swing on a branch which conveniently spread out horizontally.

At one time the bough jutted out across the lane, so that traffic had to make a diversion round it. It was long enough for the whole of the population of the village to sit on it at the same time. Then, perhaps inevitably, someone lit a fire in the middle, which reduced it to a shell.

A watercolour of Bag Enderby, painted in the 1920's, showed two cottages by the road junction here, one of them thatched. But they have long since disappeared with the ravages of time, along with most of the people. The population of the hamlet today is a mere eighteen.

SOMERSBY

Somersby is a lovely little place, its few houses clustering together at the junction of lanes by the church. To the south the small fields sweep down to a gentle valley, with just a trace of green to attract the starlings, rooks and crows to leave their nests in the December gloom. Looking across to the other side of the valley, the well trimmed hedges vanish into the mist, the trees are still and the pheasants shelter in the thickets, like infantrymen in the trenches awaiting the blitz that is to come. The fields are fairly small here, often interspersed with copses and clumps of mature trees which have survived many a winter storm.

To the north the fields are bigger, and the wider vistas are more typical of the Wold country. In the centre of the village stands the church, its squat low tower partly built of brick and partly of the inevitable greenstone, giving it the look of a well loved mongrel dog. The rough-hewn blocks of stone almost match in colour the ivy clinging to the churchyard fence, and four Scotch pine rise high above the tower as a kind of sentinel to ward off any hosts of unbelievers who may trespass along the yew tree avenue which leads to the porch.

Not that any disturber of the peace, other than a tractor or a chainsaw, ever seems the remotest possibility in Somersby. Even Cromwell's Roundheads seem to have given it a miss, for the 15 foot high 15th century churchyard cross is in a fine state of preservation. It has a castellated knob at the top of the shaft, and carvings of the Crucifixion and the Virgin and Child.

In its time it would have been used as a preaching cross by itinerant preachers, and penances would have been performed publicly in front of it. Earlier in the 20th century it was featured in Mitchell's cigarette card series on famous crosses.

The church, dedicated like that at Bag Enderby to St. Margaret, has much of interest to the historian, as well as to the devotee of Alfred, Lord Tennyson. A good deal of it is 15th century, and little details which have vanished with the ravages of time in less isolated spots are still present here. In the tower are two medieval bells, often tolled by Alfred and his brothers as boys.

If their mother had ever visited the belfry she would probably have put a stop to these exhortations to round up the parishoners, for when Henry Winn of Fulletby inspected the bells some 60 years later, in 1879, he reported:

"This church was restored about 17 years ago but no attention was paid either to the bells or the bell-chamber which is in a most dangerous state... I felt myself in great danger all the time I was at the bells, in fact my foot slipped through once. There is not stairs or ladder to reach the bells and I had to hire two men to fetch a long ladder from a farmyard. The fall door was off the hinges and we had great difficulty in preventing it from falling upon us."

There are still no stairs or ladder today, over a hundred years later. The sundial above the porch door is dated 1751 and curtly inscribed, "Time passeth."

No doubt many a congregation has been tempted to quote the words to an over-verbose rector as his sermon droned on and on

Inside the porch is a holy water stoup, normally found only in Roman Catholic or High Anglican churches, a reminder that when the church was first built we were still under the jurisdiction of Rome. The church is beautifully light, for although it is December and daylight is at a premium, the wide, plain windows and whitewashed walls make electricity superfluous. In the plain old octagonal font, Alfred and his brothers and sisters were baptised. The communion chalice, dated 1653, was referred to by Alfred in his line:

"The kneeling hamlet drains the chalice of the grapes of God."

On display are a quill pen and two clay pipes which once belonged to the poet, and a fine bronze bust of Alfred, sculptured by Thomas Woolner, was given to the church to mark the centenary of his birth. Each year a commemoration service is held, either here or at Bag Enderby, in conjunction with the Tennyson Society.

In George Clayton's time the church had a thatched roof, but it was replaced in the restoration of 1833, two years after his death. The church was again restored later in the 19th century, but the feeling of sanctity is as strong as ever. Here is a stronghold of the faith, where much earnest worship by good people has gone on through the ages.

In the sanctuary there is a memorial brass to George Littlebury who died in 1612, and next to the pulpit there are tablets to Katherine and Robert Burton, who went to their rest in 1742 and 1753 respectively.

Somersby Grange, the house with square towers and embattlements opposite the church, was built for Robert Burton in 1722. It was probably designed by the famous architect John Vanbrugh, for he often used this embattled style on his smaller buildings. It is very close in plan to the nunnery he built at Greenwich shortly before this, with four towers in the angles, each with circular and oblong windows. All the rooms are panelled and have powder closets leading off them. Some of these characteristics are to be found in Blenheim Palace, his masterpiece.

A later member of the Burton family was Langhorne Burton, who owned an estate of 11,000 acres around Somersby. Because of the agricultural depression he suffered from a severe shortage of tenants to work his land, and as rent income dropped his finances became ever more parlous. He failed to pay his church tithes to the rector, who in turn was unable to pay his parish rates. The whole area suffered, with Bag Enderby in 1879 possessing no school, no chapel, no reading room and no pub!

The rector, The Rev'd. A.B. Skipworth, was reduced to drastic means in that year to try and gather in the harvest. It was a miserably wet summer, and when the crops finally showed a damp ripeness he urged his flock to take advantage of a dry Sunday to cut and load their corn. He even took out his own cart with his sexton and a labourer, but the vehicle became bogged down in a muddy gateway and it took hours to extricate it.

Meanwhile, many of his parishioners were horrified and stood around hissing. No doubt they thought the embedded cart was an instant punishment from on high for working on the Sabbath. Many of the hissers would have been Methodists, for in this county of the Wesleys, Methodist congregations outnumbered Anglican ones by four to one, according to the religious census of 1851.

The two churches came into heated conflict in the 1870's when the Methodists strove to set up a Board School as a rival to the Church of England's National School. Langhorne Burton, a staunch supporter of the established Church, did nothing to calm matters when he threatened to evict a tenant at Bag Enderby for holding Methodist meetings in her cottage.

By the time of the 1881 census Langhorne Burton was living at The Grange in Somersby with his wife Edith and three-month-old son. He employed a general servant and a nurse, but the infant was never to inherit those 11,000 acres for his father later went bankrupt.

Next door to The Grange is the famous Rectory, where George Clayton Tennyson lived with his wife Elizabeth and their eleven children. It is a house of immense character, with its tiled roofs all at different levels and its ivy-clad front which gleams almost yellow when the sun is out. Windows peep out haphazardly as if determined not to comply with any architectural plan, and the tall chimneys are crowned by pots of different colours.

George Clayton added the Gothic hall and the gables, under one of which Alfred shared a bedroom. The dining-room had tall Gothic windows with curved heads, but the Gothic trimmings have been demolished. An upstairs balcony gives the mistress of the house all the scents of the garden as soon as she rises from her bed.

The inside of the building, once up the elegant Georgian staircase, is a warren of narrow passages and tiny rooms. Considering that the best part of two centuries have passed since the family left the house in 1837, it has not changed a great deal since Alfred wrote these lines about it one hot summer's day:

> "O joy to him in this retreat,
>   Immantled in ambrosial dark,
>   To drink the cooler air and mark
> The landscape winking through the heat:
>
> O sound to rout the brood of cares,
>   The sweep of scythe in morning dew,

And tumbled half the mellowing pears!"
The gust that round the garden flew,

There still stands a copper beech on the rectory lawn which may have been his subject when he wrote:

"Unwatched, the garden bough shall sway,
The tender blossom flutter down,
Unloved, that beech will gather brown,
This maple burn itself away."

From the hills above the village there are fine views on a clear day down the gentle valley of the River Lymn and across the marsh to the sea. Alfred's early work is full of references to the hills and valleys, and the boundless open spaces of marsh and fen. He also loved the coast around Mablethorpe and Skegness, where the family took their holidays, and where "the great waters break and thin themselves far over sand marbled with moon and cloud."

From the Tennysons' time onwards, Somersby as a village has gradually declined with the 19th century agricultural depression. As the little cottages were vacated they fell into disrepair until they finally collapsed or were demolished. Many had thatched roofs which needed constant attention.

In 1812 the population was 95, but by 1856 this had dropped to 64. The major tenant farmers in the village in the earlier half of the 19th century were the Baumbers, who lived at Manor Farm, close to the old Rectory. By 1881 the farming was in the hands of Langhorne Burton and Thomas Bagley, a young man who lived with his wife Mary and farmed 200 acres. He employed a general servant, a shepherd and a coachman.

The population had now decreased further to 43, spread over eleven houses, the chief occupations being agricultural labourers and gamekeepers. But there was a road surveyor resident in the village and also a publican. Today the population has halved again, down to a mere 21.